Friendship

Julie Murray

Abdo Kids Junior
is an Imprint of Abdo Kids
abdobooks.com

Abdo Kids
CHARACTER EDUCATION

abdobooks.com

Published by Abdo Kids, a division of ABDO, P.O. Box 398166, Minneapolis, Minnesota 55439.

Printed in the United States of America, North Mankato, Minnesota.

102019

012020

THIS BOOK CONTAINS RECYCLED MATERIALS

Photo Credits: iStock, Shutterstock

Production Contributors: Teddy Borth, Jennie Forsberg, Grace Hansen

Design Contributors: Christina Doffing, Candice Keimig, Dorothy Toth

Library of Congress Control Number: 2019941197

Publisher's Cataloging-in-Publication Data

Names: Murray, Julie, author.

Title: Friendship / by Julie Murray

Description: Minneapolis, Minnesota : Abdo Kids, 2020 | Series: Character education | Includes online resources and index.

Identifiers: ISBN 9781532188671 (lib. bdg.) | ISBN 9781644942758 (pbk.) | ISBN 9781532189166 (ebook) | ISBN 9781098200145 (Read-to-Me ebook)

Subjects: LCSH: Friendship--Juvenile literature. | Interpersonal relationships--Juvenile literature. | Feelings--Juvenile literature. | Moral ideas--Juvenile literature. |

Classification: DDC 177.62--dc23

Table of Contents

Friendship

Friendship is all around.

Do you see it?

Eric is at the park.

He plays with Bob.

Lucy needs help with math.

Adam helps her.

Grace is being **silly**.

Max laughs with her.

Chad is sad. Tom listens.

Eva scores a goal. Her team lifts her up!

Lea fell down. Mary helps her up.

Sue reads a book.

Erin and Jon join her.

What does **friendship** look like to you?

Ways to Show Friendship

celebrate with others

help others

laugh with others

listen to others

Glossary

friendship
a relationship between friends.

silly
goofy and not serious.

Index